{ Little-Known
FACTS
ABOUT
Well-Known
PLACES }

IRELAND

{ Little-Known FACTS ABOUT Well-Known PLACES
IRELAND }

David Hoffman

FALL RIVER PRESS

New York

FALL RIVER PRESS

New York

An Imprint of Sterling Publishing
387 Park Avenue South
New York, NY 10016

© 2008 by David Hoffman

This 2011 edition published by Fall River Press.

Images: jupiterimages.com

ISBN 978-1-4351-0428-0

Manufactured in the United States of America

4 6 8 10 9 7 5 3

www.sterlingpublishing.com

INTRODUCTION

Italy, Paris, New York, Ireland...
just hear their names and dozens of
familiar images come to mind. But
for everything that we may know
about these (and other) favorite
places, there is always a tidbit,
a top secret, or a twist of fate that
we have yet to discover.

   *Little-Known Facts about
Well-Known Places* goes beyond the
obvious to reveal the stories behind
the stories regarding the cities,
countries, and tourist destinations
that we all are familiar with—or at
least think we're familiar with.

Covering every aspect—from food, film, and fashion to people, history, art, and architecture—these collections of offbeat facts and figures, statistics and specifics, are guaranteed to delight a first-time visitor and surprise even the most jaded local.

Packed with a wealth of revelations that could start (or stop) a conversation—not to mention win a ton of bar bets—*Little-Known Facts about Well-Known Places* is a must-have for know-it-alls, information addicts, curious readers, armchair travelers, and pop culture junkies of all ages.

Look for these other
titles in the series:

{ Little-Known
FACTS
ABOUT
Well-Known
PLACES }

PARIS

ITALY

NEW YORK

DISNEYLAND

A good barkeep takes almost two minutes—119.5 seconds to be exact—to properly pour a pint of Guinness. One test of his expertise: if he uses the flow from the tap to draw a shamrock or write an initial in the perfectly domed head, the mark will still be visible when you drain the glass.

When Arthur Guinness opened the original Guinness Brewery in Dublin in 1759, he signed a 9,000-year lease on the property, which required a small deposit and locked in an annual rent equivalent to $85.

By the Numbers

2 BILLION
pints of Guinness sold annually worldwide

2,304,000
pints of Guinness that can be fermented
in one brewing at the company's original
St. James Gate facility in Dublin

10,000
Dubliners who are dependent on the
Guinness brewery for their livelihood;
one in every 30 residents

198
calories in a pint of Guinness; less than
a pint of skim milk or orange juice

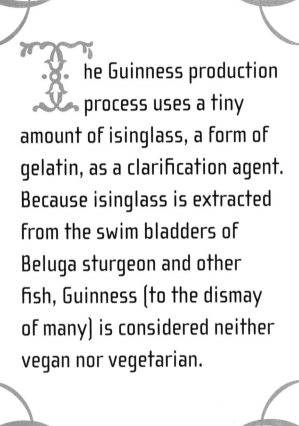

The Guinness production process uses a tiny amount of isinglass, a form of gelatin, as a clarification agent. Because isinglass is extracted from the swim bladders of Beluga sturgeon and other fish, Guinness (to the dismay of many) is considered neither vegan nor vegetarian.

The copy for the famous 1930s "animal" series of Guinness advertising posters was written by Dorothy L. Sayers, the noted mystery author. The posters, which introduced the signature Guinness toucan, were designed by John Gilroy and are still found today on pub walls all over Ireland.

Order a pint
in almost any pub in Ireland
and you will automatically
be served Guinness.

The best pint in Ireland is frequently reported to be at Mulligan's on Poolbeg Street in Dublin, where, according to folklore, its freshness is attributed to a pipe underneath the bar that connects directly to the basement of the Guinness brewery.

Guinness Stout
is always served at
room temperature.

Alcoholic drinks in
Ireland are taxed
in relation to alcohol
content, so the higher
the proof, the more
you pay.

Proper pub etiquette dictates that when someone buys you a drink, you buy him one in return. No wonder it's said that, in Ireland, it is impossible for two people to go out for just one drink.

A "drink" in Ireland implies alcohol. Everything else—soda, water, juice, coffee, tea— is a "beverage."

Ireland has the highest per-capita rate of tea consumption in the world; drinking tea is such a part of daily life that every pub is required, by law, to provide it.

By the Numbers

6

cups of tea consumed by the
average Irishman daily

10,000

pubs in Ireland
(the oldest, Sean's Bar in Athlone in
County Westmeath, opened in 900 A.D.)

210 FEET

length of the Grandstand Bar at
the Galway Race Course

457

one-ounce shots of alcohol consumed
by the average Irishman yearly

Among the most expensive drinks in the world is the mai tai served at The Bar at the Merchant Hotel in Belfast. Made with long-out-of-production 17-year aged Wray & Nephew rum (of which there are only twelve bottles in existence), the classic cocktail will set you back $1,450. Plus tip.

Temple Bar is a popular area in central Dublin, and while it is filled with theatres, music venues, nightclubs, galleries, cafes, and, yes, bars, its name has nothing to do with drinking (or practicing law, for that matter). To explain: "bar" comes from an Old English word meaning "gate," which derives from *gata*, the Norse term for "street." For many of its early years, Dublin had been occupied by Viking invaders; hence, Temple Bar was no different than saying Temple Street.

The Crown pub in Belfast is a fine example of Victorian design, although the beautifully detailed interior, with its stained glass and carved wooden booths that resemble confessionals, is more representative of a church than a bar. Original owner Patrick Flanagan took advantage of the talented Italian craftsmen who came to Northern Ireland in the late 1800s to build Catholic churches. He paid them under the table to work after hours on his saloon.

The earliest whiskey was produced by Irish monks, who called it *uisce beatha*, meaning "water of life." Its current—incorrect—pronunciation can be attributed to twelfth-century Norman soldiers from England, who loved the drink but were not so adept at speaking Gaelic. Thus *uisce* became "we-skee" instead of "ish-keh."

The first license to distill whiskey was granted to Bushmills in 1608, making it the oldest distillery in the world.

Although the distilled spirit is produced in both Ireland and Scotland, its name is spelled differently depending on its origin. If *whiskey* is spelled with an "e," it's Irish. If it's spelled without the "e" (which would be *whisky*), then it's Scotch.

Irish whiskey makers claim that their whiskey is smoother than Scotch whisky because it is distilled three times instead of two and because Irish whiskey, which by law must be aged in wooden casks for at least three years, usually ages for nine, or even twelve, years.

In 1886, the original spire of St. Malachy's Church in Belfast was removed, and the tower bell (the largest in County Ulster) was wrapped in hemp to soften its peal in response to a complaint from a nearby distillery that every time the bell tolled for Mass, it affected the maturing of their whiskey.

"Circling over Shannon" is a colloquial expression for being drunk. It came into use following Boris Yeltsin's trip to Ireland in 1994, when word spread that the Russian leader had gotten so plastered while in flight that the pilot had to circle Shannon Airport to buy him time to sober up. Only years later would it become known that the former president had not been intoxicated, but had suffered a massive heart attack.

Joe Sheridan was closing up the restaurant at Ireland's Foynes Airport in 1945 when bad weather forced a transatlantic flight to return to the airport. Sheridan greeted the tired and irritable passengers with coffee mixed with a little sugar, spiked with a shot of Irish whiskey, and topped with freshly whipped cream. When asked if what they were drinking was Brazilian coffee, Sheridan replied, "No, it's Irish Coffee." The name stuck.

Almost 5 percent of Ireland's total milk production goes to making Baileys Irish Cream liqueur.

1.05 MILLION

gallons of cream used each year
to make Baileys

40,000

cows whose sole purpose is to
supply milk to Baileys

36 HOURS

maximum amount of time allowed
after milking the cow before the milk
must be blended with whiskey
to make Baileys

24 MONTHS

shelf life of Baileys

Despite a reputation for great booze and bland food, Ireland does not lead the world in alcohol consumption (Luxembourg does), yet it does rank first in terms of calorie consumption.

Ireland eats more Corn Flakes than oatmeal—and, per capita, eats more Corn Flakes than any other country in the world.

Ireland is an island surrounded by a bounty of fresh fish, yet 75 percent of what is caught is exported. This incongruity is often attributed to the fact that for years most Irish could not eat meat on Fridays (as dictated by the Catholic church), so for them, the negative memories of being forced to have fish for dinner have left a bad taste in their mouths.

The most frequently ordered item on fast food restaurant menus in Ireland is Taco Fries. Taco Fries, a dish of chips (french fries) doused in a pink "secret sauce" and smothered with cheese, proved so popular for the Abrakebabra fast food chain when they were introduced in 2002 that it single-handedly turned around the company's dwindling sales and sparked a nationwide trend.

Champ is Irish comfort food at its best, a deceptively simple concoction of mashed potatoes and scallions cooked with milk and butter. Lots of butter. An oft-repeated story tells of a man in Cavan (the county where champ originated), who, on his deathbed, asked his wife for the one final helping of champ, only to find out that she had saved it for herself—for after his funeral.

The "classic" Irish combo of corned beef and cabbage is barely 100 years old, and is more a product of the island of Manhattan than of the Emerald Isle. Early Irish immigrants to the United States had settled on New York's  Lower East Side, and the predominantly Jewish area made finding bacon or cured ham to go with their cabbage difficult. So they did what their neighbors did—bought brisket instead, brined it in kosher salt, and served "corned beef" for dinner.

Among the more creative things the Irish did with potatoes was to use the starchy water left over after boiling them to stiffen shirt collars.

The potato is not indigenous to Ireland. How it arrived there is open for debate. One popular legend claims that the ships of the Spanish Armada were carrying potatoes and when they wrecked off the Irish coast in 1588, some of them washed ashore, but most historians agree that it was British explorer Sir Walter Raleigh who planted the first spuds in Ireland—although few concur on exactly where he did this.

$\mathcal{S}$ir Walter Raleigh might have planted the first potato in Ireland on the grounds of Killua Castle, near Clonmellon. Killua Castle was once the family seat of the Chapmans. In the 1870s, Sir Thomas Chapman had an ongoing affair with Sarah Lawrence, the governess caring for his daughters. Their relationship produced at least two children; one was Thomas Edward Lawrence, better known as Lawrence of Arabia.

In homage to Ireland and, as he put it, "to be disobedient in a way that cannot be seen," actor (and star of the film *Lawrence of Arabia*) Peter O'Toole wears only green socks, and has done so since he was fourteen years old.

In *The Quiet Man*—the film about a disgraced American boxer who retires to Ireland and finds love, directed by John Ford and starring John Wayne and Maureen O'Hara—the color green is visible somewhere in every shot, although not on anything the actors are wearing.

In 1994, the Irish government cleverly enticed actor-director Mel Gibson to shoot his Scottish epic *Braveheart* on location in Ireland rather than in Scotland by offering up, free of charge, 1,700 members of the Irish Army Reserve as extras for the film's battle scenes. A few years later, director Steven Spielberg would take a similar deal—and Ballinester Beach would stand in for Normandy in *Saving Private Ryan*.

Despite adult content and graphic violence, the Irish Film Censor gave *Michael Collins* a PG rating when it was released in 1996, due to the historical importance of its subject. The office's decision to let parents determine whether or not they wanted their kids to see the picture paid off: to date, *Michael Collins*, a biography of the twentieth-century Irish revolutionary leader, is the second most successful movie ever released in Ireland and the most successful Irish-made film of all time.

My *Left Foot*, the award-winning Irish film that told the story of painter Christy Brown, is the only movie on its initial release ever to have received an A+ rating from *Entertainment Weekly* magazine.

During the 1969 filming of *Ryan's Daughter* on the Dingle Peninsula, actor Robert Mitchum planted a small field of marijuana in a garden directly behind his hotel, and reportedly introduced much of the cast, the crew, and the town (including the police) to its use.

The Cliffs of Moher in the fishing village of Liscannor in County Clare are breathtakingly beautiful, but their rank as one of Ireland's top tourist attractions is not based on their looks alone. Movie buffs know them as the Cliffs of Insanity and flock there to see the spot where Inigo Montoya announced he was looking for the six-fingered man who killed his father in *The Princess Bride*.

Kilkenny is the only city in Ireland that is not situated on a coastline.

everal points—Emmett Square in Birr, most notably—claim to be the geographic center of Ireland. Centuries ago, however, there was no question: the only possible center (certainly the sacred center) was the Hill of Usineach, near Ballymore. From its summit you can see two-thirds of Ireland.

The Leviathan of Parsonstown in Birr was, for seventy years, the largest telescope in the world. (In 1917, it was upstaged by the Hooker Telescope at Mt. Wilson Observatory near Los Angeles.) Still operational, the Leviathan is the same telescope that Jules Verne referenced in his science fiction classic *From the Earth to the Moon*.

Counties Offaly and Westmeath were hotbeds for amateur astronomers in the nineteenth century, and both William Parsons's massive telescope in Birr and William Wilson's research at his observatory in Daramona (he was the first to measure the temperature of the sun) were defining moments in our understanding of space. Their accomplishments are all the more impressive for the same reason that Ireland never became a world center of astronomy: the weather.

250

days per year, on average, that
it is cloudy or rains in Ireland

4 HOURS,
20 MINUTES

average daily sunshine in Rosslare,
County Wexford, on the southeast
coast, the sunniest area in Ireland

90°F

highest recorded temperature
in Ireland (in 1887);
normal summer high is 78°F

Without a doubt, one of the best ways to explore the Irish landscape is by bicycle. Meteorologists recommend, particularly if you are thinking of doing this in the western counties, that you plan your route from south to north—the direction of the prevailing winds.

The work of Irish natural scientist and physicist John Tyndall from 1860 to 1880 was the foundation for twentieth-century research into the greenhouse effect and fiber optics. He conceived instruments to measure air pollution, built a respirator for firefighters, and definitively explained why the sky is blue.

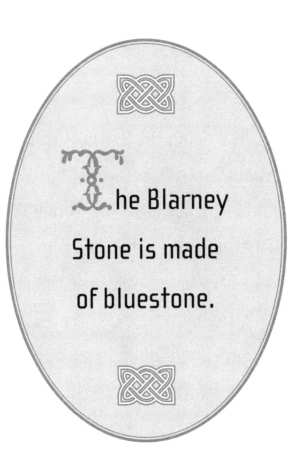

The Blarney Stone is made of bluestone.

Kissing the Blarney Stone may be an Irish tradition, but doing it is not easy. The stone is situated so that the kisser has to lie face up on the parapet walk, then lean backward over the edge, holding onto an iron railing, while someone else holds him for safekeeping.

The Blarney Stone is so named because it is located at the top of Blarney Castle. When Cormac MacCarthy, who owned the castle in the fifteenth century, managed to continually delay—with a lot of sweet talk—having to surrender the castle to Queen Elizabeth I, his skill at making convincing promises that he never made good on became known by the crown as "Blarney talk"—and in time, simply "blarney."

A V-shaped piece gouged from the underside of the Blarney Stone, which had been stolen in 1659, was found by a group of petroleum engineering students from Texas Tech in 1939. It was later installed on their campus in Lubbock, where it can still be seen today. University tradition dictates that seniors who kiss the Blarney Stone upon graduation will receive the gift of eloquent speech.

In terms of both quality and quantity, more art has been stolen from the Russborough House, a County Wicklow stately home that is now a museum outside Dublin, than any museum in the world, having been the scene of four multi-million dollar heists (with losses totaling $70 million in value) since 1974.

aravaggio's *The Taking of Christ*, assumed to be lost forever, hung anonymously in a Jesuit monastery in Dublin for sixty years. It wasn't until Sergio Bendetti, an art restorer, was brought in to clean it in the early 1990s that the painting—valued at more than $30 million—was recognized. It is currently on "indefinite loan" to Ireland's National Gallery.

One of the bathrooms inside the spectacular Lismore Castle (located midway between Waterford and Cork) is an homage to Fred Astaire, whose sister Adele married Lord Charles Cavendish, and lived with him at Lismore from 1932 to 1944.

When a fire broke out in Woodstock Castle in the thirteenth century, John Fitzgerald (the first Earl of Kildare), then an infant, was left forgotten in his room, and would have died in the blaze had a monkey, part of the royal menagerie, not carried him to safety. In appreciation, a monkey now features prominently in the Fitzgerald family coat of arms.

Ireland has
twice as many cattle
as people.

53

percent of population in Ireland
under age 35

4

percent of people in Ireland with red hair

700

Jewish families currently living in Ireland
(Chaim Herzog, president of Israel from
1983 to 1993, was the son of the chief rabbi
of Ireland and born in Belfast)

40

percent of racehorses ranked in
the Top 10 in the world that were
born and bred in Ireland

The Connemara pony is the only horse breed native to Ireland.

Colonel William Hall-Walker, founder of the celebrated horse farm in Tully that would become the Irish National Stud, attributed his success to astrology. He bred and sold foals based on their astrological signs and charts, and had skylights put into all the stables so the horses could reap the influence of sunbeams and moonlight.

Horses are an Irish passion as much as they are a tradition; there are 233 days of racing every year, on 27 racetracks.

Steeplechasing originated in Cork in 1752, with a 4.5-mile race running between Buttevant and Doneraile; the name was coined because steeples, being the tallest and most visible landmarks around, were used to mark the start and finish lines.

Eddie Hackett, Ireland's noted golf architect, designed 85 of the country's 400 courses and is celebrated for incorporating the natural dunes and rugged terrain into his designs. This was partially by choice, but also because Hackett had no other option: many of his clients were farmers looking for a way to make unproductive grazing land profitable and they could not afford bulldozers.

The Burren, a 300-square-mile weathered limestone plateau in the northwest corner of County Clare, is renowned among botanists for its varied flora and fauna, including over two dozen species of orchids. None of the flowers found here are unique to the area, but what is unique is that (thanks to the concentration of natural light, the gulf air, and the heat of the limestone) nowhere else in the world can such a wide array of plants be found growing together, side by side, in such abundance.

The longest place name in Ireland is Muckanaghederdauhaulia (in County Galway), which translates to "pig marsh between two saltwater inlets."

The gardens with the swirling motif tucked behind Dublin Castle and the Chester Beatty Library are believed to mark the spot where, centuries ago, Vikings moored their ships. The small harbor, which would not be filled in until the early 1800s, was called the Black Pool—or *Dubh Linn*. Hence, the city's name.

The world's oldest New Testament, dating from the second century, is in the Chester Beatty Library in Dublin.

1,480

authorized and numbered copies
of the Book of Kells (most are in libraries
around the world)

185

animals whose skins were used for
the vellum on which the original
Book of Kells was written

680

pages in the Book of Kells

2

undecorated pages in the Book of Kells

St. Patrick, whose real name was believed to be Maewyn Succat, was Welsh, not Irish. It is not known if March 17 was the date of his birth, or his death.

In Ireland, March 17 has always been a national holiday, but for the most part, a religious one; a time for quiet reflection. In fact, it was only as recently as the 1970s that the pubs were open, and it was not until the mid-1990s that Ireland (literally) joined the parade and launched what has become the largest celebration of St. Patrick in the world.

Like parades, green beer, green bagels, and dyed green rivers are a decidedly Irish-American take on St. Patrick's Day. Customarily, the only green the Ireland Irish wear on St. Patrick's Day is a sprig of shamrock, usually in the lapel of a jacket or coat.

Snakes are not native to Ireland. St. Patrick may get credit for ridding the country of snakes, but the truth is they were never there.

It is highly unlikely that St. Patrick ever explained the concept of the Holy Trinity to a non-believer using a shamrock. There was not only no written record of this theory until 1727 (more than one thousand years after Patrick's death), but even the first-ever mention of the shamrock in the dictionary only dates back to the late sixteenth century.

IRELAND
FACTS

The widespread use in Ireland of Patrick as a boy's name really did not begin until the early eighteenth century, so its popularity is believed to be due to lieutenant-general and war hero Patrick Sarsfield and the country's fascination with him at the time more than it is to the patron saint.

While Gaelic-rooted baby names are becoming more widespread in Ireland, Jack and Sarah are currently the most popular names for newborn children. The most common surname is Murphy.

At fourteen, Marie Louise O'Murphy left her parents' home in Cork to become a model at the Paris Academy of Painting, where she posed for Francois Boucher (that's her in his noted portrait *Girl Resting*) prior to catching the eye of Louis XV and going off to live at Versailles as his mistress. Legend has it that the money she regularly sent back to her relatives ultimately provided the next generation with capital to launch the family business: Murphy's Ale.

The Celtic harp—not the shamrock—is the national symbol of Ireland. The harp depicted on government seals, coins, passports, and the Leinster flag belonged to Brian Boru, who, as High King of Ireland from 1002 to 1014, had the harp played to rally his troops. The original can be found in the museum at Trinity College, Dublin.

The colors of Ireland's national flag break down as follows: green represents people of native Irish ancestry; orange signifies the descendants of the seventeenth-century British colonists; white in the center symbolizes the hope for reconciliation between the two.

86

IRELAND
FACTS

The Red Hand of Ulster, the ancient Celtic symbol that now represents Northern Irish Protestant identity, reportedly originated when two chieftains were fighting each other to rule Ulster. They decided to settle their dispute with a race; the one whose hand touched Ulster first would be the new king. When they reached the river that fronted the province, one swam across, while the other took out his sword, cut off his hand, and threw it onto the opposite bank. Thus, he claimed that he was the first to touch Ulster, and would be king.

In the late-1800s, the Ulster Overcoat Company, based in Belfast, released its namesake design. Made specifically for traveling, the Ulster came either double- or single-breasted, had a cape, and reached almost to the ankles. The garment became recognizable worldwide after Sir Arthur Conan Doyle dressed his fictional detective Sherlock Holmes in one.

At their March 5, 1971, concert at Ulster Hall in Belfast, rock group Led Zeppelin performed their iconic *Stairway to Heaven* for the first time. Reportedly, when they announced they were going to play it, the crowd was not responsive to hearing a new song—until they heard it.

Even without touring, and despite the fact that her only live performances have been a handful of TV appearances, Irish singer-songwriter Enya has sold more than 70 million albums.

ixing traditional Irish music with punk, the Pogues originally called themselves Pogue Mahone, which is Gaelic for "kiss my ass." They were forced to shorten their name when the BBC refused to play the band's first single unless they did.

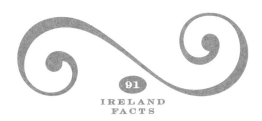

Irish step-dancing (now recognizable worldwide, thanks to *Riverdance*) was created after the British conquest in the 1600s outlawed music, and cultural traditions had to be performed in secret. The dance form that evolved—body and arms kept stationary, movement confined to the feet—ensured that if the English glanced at the locals through a window, they would be unable to tell that anyone was dancing.

The first performance of *Riverdance* was developed in 1994 as a one-time thing—an act to entertain the audience during an intermission in the ESC (the Eurovision Song Contest), which Dublin was hosting that year.

Before it became synonymous with step-dancing, the word *riverdance* was (and still is) a colloquial term for the act of committing suicide in the Shannon River.

U2 drummer Larry Mullen was a member of the Artane Boys Band, the marching band that plays before and during every major sports event at Dublin's Croke Park (and has since the late 1880s). His experience with them inspired the rumbling, militaristic beats he plays on many U2 songs, including the band's signature *Sunday Bloody Sunday*.

Bono is the only person who has been nominated for an Oscar, a Grammy, a Golden Globe—and a Nobel Peace Prize.

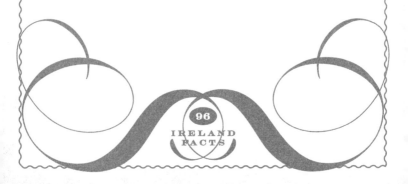

Poets were rock stars in ancient Ireland; with no books or media available, it was left to them to preserve the history of the royals and inform the country.

In the eighteenth century, the poets of the Maigue Valley would stage festivals at Croom in County Limerick, where for fun, they challenged each other to create humorous, off-the-cuff, and sometimes off-color five-line verses. These became known as "limericks."

Poet William Butler Yeats was mockingly nicknamed the "Gland Old Man" by Dublin newspapers in 1934 after he went to Vienna and (at the age of 69) underwent the Steinach operation, a surgical procedure that promised to renew his creative and sexual drives. Yeats had the last laugh: in the five years that followed, he would become editor of *The Oxford Book of Modern Verse* and take on three lovers.

William Drennan was a successful Belfast obstetrician who advocated smallpox vaccination and hand-washing to prevent the spread of infection. He was also a poet; and his poem *When Erin First Rose* was the first to call Ireland the "Emerald Isle."

Let no feeling of vengeance presume to defile/The cause of, or men of, the Emerald Isle.

In 1844, Dublin physician Francis Rynd pricked a small hole in a patient's face and inserted in it a narrow tube, through which he trickled morphine solution so that the drug flowed underneath the skin and directly into the bloodstream. The procedure proved less painful and more effective than the oral medication of the day, and led to the development of the hypodermic syringe and intravenous therapy.

William Wilde, the father of Oscar Wilde, was so skilled an ear surgeon that a procedure he perfected (now known as Wilde's Incision) is still performed today.

James Joyce's masterwork *Ulysses*, which follows the character Leopold Bloom through Dublin over a period of twenty-four hours, is set on June 16, 1904—the same day that the author began his relationship with his future wife, Nora Barnacle.

3

museums in Dublin devoted
solely to James Joyce

5

wristwatches James Joyce wore
on his arm simultaneously; each
was set to a different time zone

$445,000

price paid at auction for an
erotic letter James Joyce sent
to Nora Barnacle

Judging by the torrid letters he wrote to Nora Barnacle, James Joyce may not have had issues with whips and chains, but he was freaked out by puppies. As a child, he was bitten by a stray—and the fear stayed with him.

Playwright Samuel Beckett's first writing job was as James Joyce's assistant; he transcribed every line of *Finnegans Wake* as Joyce, whose eyesight was failing, dictated.

One day, while James Joyce was dictating *Finnegans Wake* to Samuel Beckett, there was an unexpected knock on the door. Joyce called out "Come in." Beckett hadn't heard the knock but he did hear Joyce, and dutifully transcribed the author's every word. When Joyce later discovered the accidental line in his manuscript, he liked the way it sounded and left it in the finished book.

Whenever James Joyce went out with friends, he would surreptitiously jot down phrases from their conversations on scraps of paper. Once back home, he would sort through them and use his friends' words as dialog in his novels.

merican physicist Murray Gell-Mann dubbed the three subatomic particles he discovered "quarks," an homage to an expression James Joyce had coined to describe the three distinct sounds made by seabirds in book 2, episode 4 of *Finnegans Wake*.

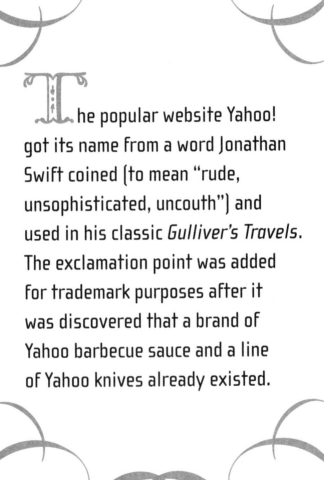

The popular website Yahoo! got its name from a word Jonathan Swift coined (to mean "rude, unsophisticated, uncouth") and used in his classic *Gulliver's Travels*. The exclamation point was added for trademark purposes after it was discovered that a brand of Yahoo barbecue sauce and a line of Yahoo knives already existed.

Jonathan Swift was a regular visitor to Gaulston House, a long-gone estate that stood on the shores of Lough Ennell in County Westmeath. During his daily walks on the grounds, Swift noticed how miniscule the people on the opposite side of the lake appeared, an observation that would later inspire the tiny Lilliputians in *Gulliver's Travels*.

Thomas Lefroy would grow up to be a noted judge and politician and, for fourteen years, the Chief Justice of Ireland, but as a young man he so charmed author Jane Austen that she modeled the character of Mr. Darcy in *Pride and Prejudice* after him.

George Bernard Shaw moved to England when he was twenty, but he was forever a wily Irishman. He purposefully named the secluded studio behind his house, where he wrote many of his major works, after the British capital, so whenever unwanted visitors called, they could be told that he was not available—because he was "in London."

As a kid, C.S. Lewis moved into Little Lea, a house that his father had built (and that still stands) on Circular Road in east Belfast. There, he discovered a giant, free-standing clothing wardrobe, that would inspire him to not only dream up make-believe worlds at age seven, but again at age fifty-two, when he wrote *The Lion, the Witch, and the Wardrobe*.

IRELAND
FACTS

Rare for any city, but particularly for one of only 500,000 people, Belfast has three daily newspapers: the *Irish News*, *Belfast Telegraph*, and *News Letter*. The *News Letter* was first published in 1737 and is the oldest English-language general daily newspaper still in publication in the world.

Since 1969, artists, writers, composers, and sculptors living in Ireland have been exempt from paying income tax.

In the seventeenth century, when the residents of Ireland successfully blocked a proposed income tax (claiming that disclosing financial records was a violation of personal rights), the government implemented a glass tax instead, which was computed based on the number of windows in a home. Officials figured the more windows someone had, the bigger the house; and the bigger the house, the more money they made. It also explains why so many houses from that period had bricked-up windows.

Ireland's president Mary McAleese is not a citizen of Ireland. Born into a Catholic family in Belfast, she is technically British; however, Irish law stipulates that a resident of Northern Ireland is permitted to hold political office in the Republic of Ireland.

Mary McAleese followed President Mary Robinson, marking the first time anywhere in the world that two women have served in succession as an elected head of state.

Kilkenny-born architect James Hoban designed the original White House in Washington, D.C., after winning a competition (in which he defeated Thomas Jefferson for the job) in 1792. Hoban based his design on Richard Cassels's Leinster House in Dublin, but at George Washington's request, modified the number of stories from three to two for economic reasons.

One-third of the homes currently standing in Ireland were built in the last decade.

A long-held superstition in Ireland is that if you move on a Saturday, disaster is sure to follow. This not only applies to moving to a new residence, but also to coming home from the hospital or going on vacation.

The RMS *Titanic* was built and launched at the Harland and Wolff shipyard in Belfast. During the fitting out process, chief designer Alexander Carlisle announced that it would be possible to equip the vessel with 64 lifeboats, which would have provided more than enough seats for everybody on board. But because only 16 were legally required, White Star, the owner of the Titanic, cut the number to 32, and then again to 20, explaining that too many lifeboats would "sully the aesthetic beauty of the ship."

$7.5 MILLION
cost to build the *Titanic* in 1912
(about $400 million by today's
economic standards)

15,000
workers hired to build the *Titanic*

$10
average weekly salary of laborers
hired to build the *Titanic*

4
months laborers would have needed
to work to afford one first-class ticket
on the *Titanic*

reland's 1996 Olympic gold medal swimmer Michelle Smith was banned from the sport in 1998 after her urine sample was found to be so full of alcohol (presumably to hide any traces of performance enhancing drugs) that it could have been given a proof rating.

IRELAND
FACTS

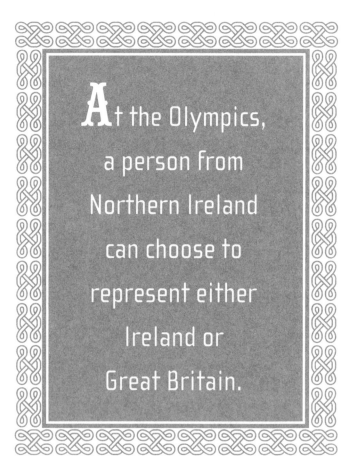

At the Olympics, a person from Northern Ireland can choose to represent either Ireland or Great Britain.

The 11,000 uniformed members of the Garda Síochána, Ireland's national police, do not carry firearms. The force's sole defense weapon is a lightweight, retractable baton, which in 2007 replaced the wooden truncheons that had been a staple since the 1800s.

IRELAND

reland is a
neutral state and is
not a member of NATO.

The Court House in Carlow is perhaps the finest neoclassical building in Ireland, yet its architectural splendor is surprising considering Carlow is a tiny country town of 20,000 people. One explanation for this: the elaborate granite structure was actually intended for the larger city of Cork (and Cork's small court house was supposed to be built in Carlow), but the plans were similar (both feature a portico and ten columns) and were inadvertently mixed up.

Ireland has the second highest number of lawyers per capita in the world, after the United States.

It is against the law to buy molasses in Sligo without a license. This is a legal hangover from the days when the county was the poteen capital of Ireland. (Poteen is a highly potent form of "moonshine" and molasses is one of its key ingredients.) Should the law ever be enforced it could prove problematic to those who ascribe to the old Irish folk remedy that a daily dose of molasses, melted in water and taken by the spoonful like medicine, will prevent varicose veins.

Irish monks fermented mead—an alcoholic brew of honey, water, and yeast—for medicinal purposes, but began to call it "honey wine" when they found that it was not just sick people who felt no pain after drinking it. In time, a bottle of honey wine became a traditional gift for a bride and groom, to be shared "for one full moon after they were married." Hence the term "honeymoon."

It was customary at ancient Irish weddings for a couple's clasped hands to be tied together by rope as a visual representation of their union, which could explain why getting married is often referred to as "tying the knot."

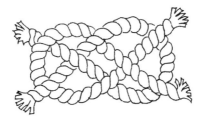

Until the 1920s, it was wise to watch where you were walking in Teltown on St. Brigid's Day. Apparently, all it took for a couple to be legally wed on that one day was to simply walk toward each other. If the pair decided the relationship was not going to work out, they only had to show up (same place, same day, a year later) and walk away from each other—and the marriage would officially be over.

Divorce was banned in
Ireland in 1937 (until 1995),
but years earlier, enlightened
Celts allowed that stealing, lying
about your love life, or sexual
impotence brought on by a partner's
obesity were all valid grounds
for ending a marriage.

In Ireland, condoms were known by religious zealots as "sheaths of Satan" and it was not until 1985 that they became available without a prescription.

In an attempt to avoid the consequences of having sex, many young people, unable to get around the state's ban on condoms that was still in effect in the 1980s, resorted to using plastic wrap as a contraceptive.

Since 1745, more than 300,000 babies have been born at The Rotunda, in Dublin, the first (and still the longest continually operating) maternity hospital in the world.

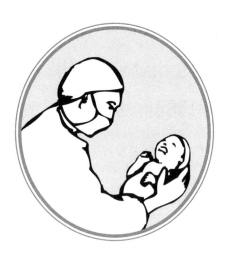

2.7465

average number of kids per family
in Ireland today

10

average number of kids per family in Ireland
from the 1940s through the 1960s

1,600

prostitutes working the Monto, Dublin's
red light district in its heyday from the
1860s to the 1900s

50,000

current members of Dublin's Pioneer Total
Abstinence Association

The term "deflowering," in reference to a girl's loss of virginity, came out of an Ireland school exercise in which a nun would hold up a daisy, pull the petals off one by one, then challenge a student in the class to reattach them. They couldn't, of course; just as they couldn't get their virginity back once they had given it up.

The small town of Ringaskiddy in County Cork is also known as Viagra Falls; it has been home to Pfizer's Viagra plant since the mid-1990s.

A legendary social gaffe supposedly occurred during a government function at Stormont in the 1920s, when Dawson Bates, Northern Ireland's Minister of Home Affairs, entered the parliament building with his wife and young son. As the three made their way through the room, their arrival was trumpeted: "the honorable Dawson Bates, his wife, Lady Bates, and their son Master Bates."

Dubliners have a penchant for humanizing statues, monuments, and landmarks by giving them irreverent nicknames. The 390-foot-high Spire of Dublin on O'Connell Street may officially be known as the Monument of Light, but it has myriad more colorful monikers. Among them: the Skewer in the Sewer, Stiletto in the Ghetto, Spire in the Mire, Spike in the Dyke, Poker near Croker, Erection at the Intersection, Stiffy by the Liffey, Nail in the Pale, and Milligan (after the comedian, Spike).

Famous Dubliners with statues erected in their honor are not immune from the locals' love of rhyming, comic nicknames. On North Earl Street, James Joyce stands with his cane and is fondly known as the Prick with the Stick. Oscar Wilde sits on a rock in Merrion Square Park; some have dubbed him the Quare in the Square or the Fag on the Crag. And the Molly Malone statue on Grafton Street, which depicts the beautiful fishmonger in a low-cut dress, has given way to numerous catcalls: the Tart with the Cart, the Dish with the Fish, and the Trollop with the Scallops.

There are at least
five different accents
in Dublin alone.

The small gold or silver ring-shaped pin worn by people throughout Ireland is known as a *fáinne*; sporting one indicates that you can and will speak Irish.

Currently, there are eight times as many people in Ireland who speak Polish as people who speak Gaelic.

The demand for Irish-speaking schools has boomed in the last decade. More than 65 Gaelscoils have opened since 2000; all have them have waiting lists.

J, K, Q, V, W, X, Y, and Z

are not used in the Irish

alphabet, which only has

18 letters.

There are no direct translations for "yes" or "no" in the Irish language, which could explain why the Irish always respond to a direct question with an explanation.

In Irish, the word for "men" is *fir* and the word for "women" is *mna*. Simple enough. Except in some parts of the country this could mean that the restroom door for males will be marked with an F while the restroom for females might be identified with an M. Oops.

"**F**ecking" is definitely intended to be used as an Irish alternative to a swear word, but not the one most people think. Despite the way it sounds, it does not have the same meaning as f**king, nor is it as offensive; a better equivalent would be the British "bloody."

Irish slang for body parts includes "bradleys" for underarms (from Brad Pitt) and "ronnie" for a mustache (after the movie star Ronald Coleman, who was immediately recognizable from his).

You will rarely, if ever, find the Irish saying, "Top o' the morning…" That expression was made up by screenwriters Edmund Beloin and Richard Breen for the 1949 Bing Crosby movie of the same name.

In 1791, James Daly, a theater manager, bet that he could introduce a nonsense word and make it known within 24 hours. He had the word scribbled in chalk on walls all over Dublin, but there was one problem: the word was "quiz," and unbeknownst to Daly, it was already a little-used word meaning "odd" or "eccentric." Regardless, Daly's stunt had people asking "What's a quiz?" The fact that the word "quiz" had become synonymous with something that begged for answers led to its present day meaning.

The word "galore"
comes from the Irish
go leor, which means
"enough" or "plenty."

When someone has had enough, they might be told to "Say uncle!" This comes from the Irish *anacal*, meaning "have mercy."

The term "dude" is an anglicized version of an Irish expression; it stems from the word *dúid* meaning "foolish-looking fellow."

The phrase "by hook or by crook" is commonly attributed to British Lord Protector Oliver Cromwell, who debated whether to approach Waterford Harbour by way of Hook Head on the one side or via the village of Crooke, on the other.

It is a common misconception that the surname prefix "Mc" is Irish and "Mac" is Scottish. In truth, "Mc" is simply an abbreviation of "Mac" and both forms, which are Gaelic for "son," are used by both nationalities. Hence, MacDonald (or McDonald) is literally "son of Donald."

The classic hand-knitted Irish fisherman's sweater is called an Aran, and comes from the Aran Islands located at the mouth of Galway Bay. The oft-told tale that Aran knitting is an ancient traditional craft and that the distinct patterns and centuries-old designs represent individual families (in the same vein as Scottish plaids) is an Irish yarn; the story, it turns out, was fabricated solely as a marketing tool. In truth, Aran sweaters, while beautifully crafted, have only been made since the 1930s.

By the Numbers

2.5 POUNDS
minimum weight of an Aran sweater

10
different stitches used to make
one Aran sweater

4 TO 6
texture patterns incorporated into one
Aran sweater (each 2 to 4 inches wide,
and running the length of the sweater
in columns from top to bottom)

$250
average cost of a hand-knitted
Aran sweater

The popularity of both Aran sweaters and Waterford Crystal in the United States can be traced back to the early 1960s and John F. Kennedy, whose presidency created an interest in, and a demand for, all things Irish.

The sparkling crystal ball that drops in New York's Times Square on New Year's Eve features hundreds of custom-designed crystals made by Ireland's famed Waterford Crystal.

1,212 POUNDS

weight of the Times Square
New Year's Eve Ball

672

triangular-shaped Waterford Crystal pieces
that comprised the 2008 Times Square
New Year's Eve Ball, created in honor of
the 100th Times Square ball-drop

186

Waterford patterns currently available

5

years one must apprentice to qualify as
a Waterford cutter

Attention Shoppers: The small shamrock sometimes printed next to an item—in particular, a food item—listed on your sales receipt indicates that the item was made or grown in Ireland.

Not only do 300 major electronics companies develop, market, and manufacture in Ireland, but because the country serves as the place of departure for all shipments to Europe and the Middle East, it is currently the largest exporter of software products in the world.

According to a recent Bank of Ireland report, Ireland has the world's second-highest wealth per capita (and over 33,000 millionaires), ahead of the United States, the United Kingdom, France, and Germany, but behind Japan.

Money may not grow on trees, but there is a belief in Ireland that hammering a coin into the bark of a tree will bring good luck (not unlike tossing a coin into a fountain and making a wish). The only problem is that the trees, much like the one on the Tyrone shore of Lough Neagh, can become so completely covered in coins that they eventually die from metal poisoning.

It is not uncommon to see hawthorn trees, especially the ones found near holy wells throughout the Irish countryside, covered in torn pieces of old clothing. It is thought that any problem or illness suffered by the person whose scrap of clothing has been tied to these "rag trees" will disappear as the rag rots away.

In Gaelic folklore, hawthorn trees have strong ties to fairies and mark the entrance to their world. A hawthorn in bloom is traditionally cut and decorated as a May bush, but to chop one down when it is not flowering is said to bring bad luck. Some Irish attribute the failure of the DeLorean Motor Company to the fact that a giant hawthorn that grew on the site of the company's Dunmurry manufacturing plant was bulldozed during construction.

iding a pot
of gold may be what
leprechauns are best known
for, but it is not their full-time
job; by trade they are the
official shoemakers of the
fairy kingdom.

Kildare Cathedral, built in 1223 on the site where St. Brigid is supposed to have founded her first convent, had fallen into ruin by the middle of the nineteenth century. Augustus Frederick Fitzgerald, the 3rd Duke of Leinster, was so determined to save the historic structure that he took it upon himself to raise the funds to rebuild it, and so would take off and travel the country—dressed as a beggar. The monies he collected eventually paid for the restoration of the building.

Until the late 1990s, RTE, Ireland's most popular television network, featured an image of St. Brigid's cross in either its logo or hidden within its station IDs (even though the station was not affiliated with the church and carried a wide range of programming).

Six One, the quirky title for the evening news seen on RTE in Ireland, comes from the fact that, since the 1950s, the public television network has stopped broadcasting at six o'clock nightly for a one-minute period of (what is now) ecumenical prayer. Because of this, the broadcast does not officially start until 6:01 P.M.—hence the name.

Among the ruins in Clonmacnoise, a monastic site on a rise above the Shannon River in County Offaly, is a dramatic fifteenth-century archway that was built into the walls of the cathedral and which doubled as a confessional. The acoustics of the arch were such that lepers could stand inside it and have their sins heard by a priest (who was positioned elsewhere in the building) without infecting him.

wo of the smaller structures still standing at Clonmacnoise—Kieran's Church and the Nun's Church—are secretly connected by an underground tunnel. Because the Vikings never attacked the nuns, the priests constructed the passageway so that when they were attacked, they had a clandestine means through which they could transport their treasures out of the monastery for safekeeping.

easuring only 12 feet by
6 feet (and totaling 72 square feet),
St. Gobhan's Church at Portbraddan,
a tiny fishing village with six houses
near Ballycastle, is the smallest
church in Ireland—and possibly,
the smallest church in the world.

A piece of stone from each of Ireland's 32 counties was used in the construction of St. Anne's Cathedral in Belfast.

The Newgrange passage tomb in the Boyne Valley was constructed around 3200 B.C., which makes it 1,000 years older than Stonehenge and 500 years older than the pyramids. Even more amazing: it wasn't until the late seventeenth century—when the prehistoric site was unearthed during an excavation of rock and stone for road pavement—that anyone even knew it was there.

Newgrange was built as a tomb for kings, but it was also designed to catch the sun at specific times of the year—particularly during the winter solstice and the spring or fall equinox—and as a calendar, it is astonishingly accurate.

By the Numbers

15 YEARS

waiting time for tickets to view the winter solstice at Newgrange before the lottery system was instituted in 2000

28,000

names entered into the Newgrange winter solstice lottery annually

100

total tickets available to view the winter solstice (20 per day for 5 days)

4 MINUTES

time after sunrise that the winter solstice occurs

17 MINUTES

daily duration of the winter solstice

ot as visited (or as well-known) as Newgrange, but according to locals, the best-kept archaeological secret in Ireland, is the large group of burial chambers at Loughcrew. There are no tour buses, no guides, no entrance fees; just stone structures that date back more than 6,000 years and are believed to be the oldest man-made dwellings on the planet.

The greatest distance between any two points in Ireland is 302 miles. However, if all of the stone walls from the country's neolithic and megalithic sites were lined up end to end, they would stretch for a quarter of a million miles.

Sheela-na-Gigs are figurative, ancient stone carvings of naked women, depicted with their legs apart to reveal their genitals. Although the original intent was not erotic (most likely, they were symbols of birth or fertility), puritan Ireland would later consider the pose obscene. The irony is that Ireland has the greatest number of known Sheela-na-Gigs found anywhere (101 of them; the best example is in the Round Tower at Rattoo)—most are found above the windows or doorways of churches.

By the 1950s, censorship in Ireland was so severe that the Church actually hired a staff whose sole purpose was to cut pictures of lingerie out of foreign publications coming into the country.

In 1907, *The Playboy of the Western World* by J.M. Synge famously caused rioting in the Abbey Theatre's auditorium. Dublin audiences were offended by the mention of the word "shift" (a woman's undergarment) and the depiction on stage of a prostitute.

 hen the Abbey Theatre
opened in Dublin in 1904, part
of the building that housed it
had previously functioned as
the city morgue.

Dublin's Mountjoy Prison is a protected structure so when it shuts down in 2011  (after a new facility opens), it cannot be torn down. The government plans to repurpose the property… as a boutique hotel.

In a unique arrangement established through Opera Ireland, all of the sets and costumes used in their 2006 production of *La Bohème* at the Gaiety Theatre in Dublin were made by inmates at Mountjoy Prison.

If you roll a stone along the parapet on either side of the bridge over the Owenmore River in Bellacorrick, musical notes will be produced in rapid succession. You can also hold the stone in your hand and strike it against each slab as you walk pass. Each hit will result in a different note and combine to create a melodic scale.

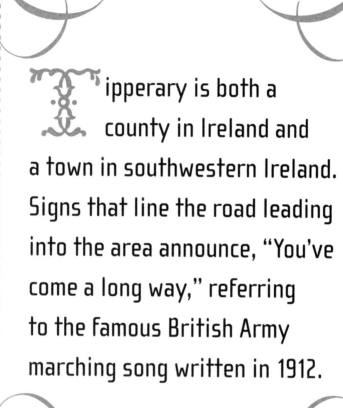

Tipperary is both a county in Ireland and a town in southwestern Ireland. Signs that line the road leading into the area announce, "You've come a long way," referring to the famous British Army marching song written in 1912.

Jack Judge was a British music hall entertainer when he came up with *It's a Long Way to Tipperary*—a result of a bet (he'd been challenged to pen a song in a day) and a conversation he overheard between two men leaving the club after hours ("It's a long way to Connemara," one had said). The rhythmic line struck a chord, and with a slight tweak, Jack won the wager—and had a hit tune on his hands.

Although recognized and regarded as an Irish ballad, *I'll Take You Home Again, Kathleen* was written by Thomas Westendorf, a public school music teacher in Plainfield, Indiana. Westendorf created the tune for his wife (who actually was named Jeanie), when she was away and visiting her hometown—of Ogdensburg, New York.

While *Danny Boy* is considered an Irish anthem, it is actually one of more than a hundred songs that have been composed using the same tune, *Londonderry Air*.

Songwriters Frederick Weatherly (who wrote the lyrics for *Danny Boy*), Jack Judge (*It's a Long Way to Tipperary*), and Thomas Westendorf (*I'll Take You Home Again, Kathleen*) never set foot in Ireland.

ABOUT THE AUTHOR

David Hoffman is a television writer, a frequent on-camera correspondent, and the author of over a dozen books about popular culture, for which, in recent years, he has been paid to play with toys, challenge untapped cooking skills (with the help of some big-name chefs), and eat and shop his way across the country. He lives in Los Angeles, where he likes to pretend this is hard work.

DISCLAIMER

All facts, figures, statistics, stories, quotes, and anecdotes found on these pages were checked (and double-checked) and believed to be true (or have some semblance of truth) at the time the book went to press. But things change; stuff happens. So cut me some slack if they're not.